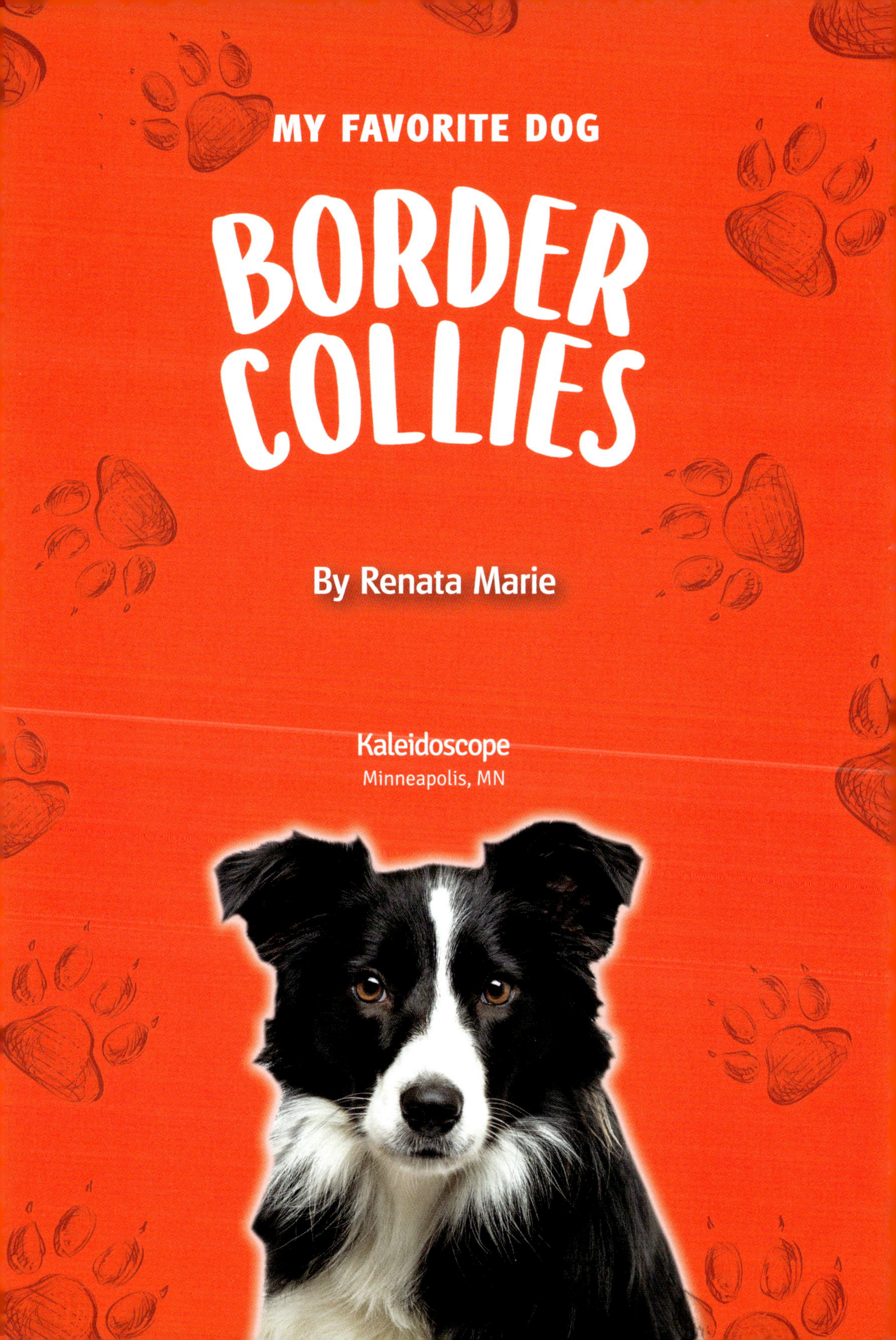

MY FAVORITE DOG

BORDER COLLIES

By Renata Marie

Kaleidoscope
Minneapolis, MN

The Quest for Discovery Never Ends

This edition first published in 2022 by Kaleidoscope Publishing, Inc.

For information regarding permission, write to
Kaleidoscope Publishing, Inc.
6012 Blue Circle Drive
Minnetonka, MN 55343

Library of Congress Control Number
2021934895

ISBN
978-1-64519-471-2 (library bound)
978-1-64519-479-8 (ebook)

Printed in the United States of America.

FIND ME
IF YOU CAN!

Bigfoot lurks within one of the images in this book. It's up to you to find him!

TABLE OF CONTENTS

Introduction

What a Catch!

"Ready, Trix?" Sophie's Border Collie spins in a circle. It's a sunny summer day at the dog park. Sophie has been practicing throwing a frisbee farther. Now it's time to see if Trix can catch it. Sophie runs, draws back, and releases the frisbee. "Fetch!" she yells.

Trix takes off. The frisbee sails across the park. Trix is right behind it. Other dogs take notice of the frisbee, but Trix is faster. The frisbee starts to drop. Trix leaps! She catches it! "Way to go, Trix!" Sophie calls. Trix wags her tail as she returns the frisbee. "Again?" Sophie asks. Trix barks. *She could play all day!* Sophie thinks.

Chapter 1

The Story of Border Collies

A Border Collie sits on a rock and watches over a flock of sheep. The mountains in the Scottish Highlands can be dangerous. He needs to keep the flock together. A lamb strays from the flock. It nears a cliff. The Border Collie acts quickly! He cuts the lamb off and guides it to safety.

The Border Collie's **instinct** to herd goes back to ancient times when people fought over England. His **ancestors** were big, strong herding dogs from the Roman Empire and tiny, quick herding dogs from the Vikings. Both breeds stayed in England after their people left. They mixed and created the Border Collie.

A Shetland Sheepdog

A German Shepherd

Some Border Collies still herd **livestock**. Dog breeds are put into groups. Border Collies are in the Herding Group. Dogs in the Herding Group are bred to control the movement of animals. A few other dogs in this group include German Shepherd Dogs, Pembroke Welsh Corgis, and Shetland Sheepdogs.

Border Collies like Trix are very smart and can be trained easily. That's why they're the top dogs of many herding, obedience, and agility competitions.

A Pembroke Welsh Corgi

TOP DOG

In agility competitions, dogs run and jump through an obstacle course at the commands of their handlers. Since the 1970s, when the competition began, Border Collies have **dominated** the course. A Border Collie named P!nk won the 2020 Westminster Kennel Club agility competition. She won against hundreds of dogs.

Trix doesn't compete in dog sports, but she does get plenty of exercise! Sophie takes her to the dog park every day and teaches her tricks at home. An active Border Collie is a happy Border Collie.

Border Collies are often used to help find missing people. A Border Collie's intelligence and strong sense of smell make it a quick and helpful search and rescue dog.

Where BORDER COLLIES come from

Chapter 2

Looking at a Border Collie

Sophie waves the frisbee in front of Trix. Trix's eyes never leave the frisbee. Like other Border Collies, Trix is focused when she works or plays. "Sit," Sophie says. Trix sits. Sophie steps back. "Stay." Trix stays. Sophie runs forward and launches the frisbee. "Fetch!" Trix is off! Her fur sweeps to her sides as she flies after the frisbee.

Border Collies can come in many different colors. Some have blue merle fur. It has patches of white, brown, and blue. The blue fur looks gray. Border Collies can also have a solid coat or a coat with a mixture of colors like black, blue, gold, red, sable, which has black-tipped hairs, brindle, which is brown and black stripes, or even lilac. All Border Collies usually have white markings on their fur with a mixture of other spots, too.

FUN FACT

The most common Border Collie colors are chocolate and white, black and white, and tricolor.

THE

BORDER COLLIE

MALES

HEIGHT:*
19-22 inches (48-56 cm)

WEIGHT:
30-55 pounds (14-25 kg)

FEMALES

HEIGHT:*
18-21 inches (46-53 cm)

WEIGHT:
30-55 pounds (14-25 kg)

**The height of a dog is measured from the top of the shoulder, not from the top of the head.*

HEAD
Sloped smoothly to nose
EARS
Medium-sized, tips fall forward
EYES
Oval, alert, intelligent, eager
CHEST
Deep, medium-broad
PAWS
Oval, medium arch, deep and strong pads

Sophie's frisbee loses its spin. It starts to curve and fall, but Trix is quick on her feet! She makes the sharp turn and leaps for a catch. It's two for two! "Good girl, Trix!" Sophie calls. When Trix runs, she's so fast that she looks like a streak of white and gray. Her **gait** is graceful. She's **agile**. She also has a lot of **endurance**. That's why she can stay under a frisbee that flies far. Sophie loves watching Trix run for frisbees.

Some dogs have light, longer fur called feathers. Border Collies have feathered forelegs, haunches, chests, and undersides.

Chapter 3

Meet a Border Collie!

"What a mess!" Sophie says as she opens the front door. Stinky gym clothes are all over the living room floor, and tissues litter the couch. "Want to help me clean?" she asks Trix. Trix wags her tail. Cleaning is a game to her. "Tidy up, Trix!" Trix bounds into the room and gathers the tissues into a pile. Sophie sweeps them into the trash. Trix picks up a sock. "Laundry," Sophie says. Trix runs in and out of the laundry room until the clothes are all in the washer. Sophie starts the wash. "We make a great team, Trix!" Trix and other Border Collies are happy to help their humans. They also love to learn new tricks.

Because they are so smart, Border Collies need to be trained right away or they'll learn bad habits.

FUN FACT

Many famous people have owned Border Collies, including Queen Victoria, Robert Burns, Anna Paquin, Bon Jovi, and Tiger Woods.

The doorbell rings just as they finish cleaning. Sophie's parents are having friends over. Trix barks but hides behind Sophie. Border Collies can be shy around new people. They were bred to herd animals, not protect them. They can be watchdogs, but they don't act as guard dogs.

Before long, Trix is playing with the visitors. It takes her a while to warm up to new people, but when she does, Sophie thinks she's the sweetest pup!

WHAT A TRICK!

Border Collies are experts at breaking records. A Border Collie named Chaser was widely recognized as the smartest dog in the world. She was able to name more than one thousand objects! Jumpy, another Border Collie, holds a Guinness World Record for skateboarding 328 feet (100 meters) in less than twenty seconds. Striker is a Border Collie that can roll down a **manual** car window. Sweat Pea balanced a can on her head while walking 328 feet only two minutes and 55 seconds. Now those are tricky tricks!

Chapter 4

Caring for a Border Collie

Trix nudges her bowl toward Sophie. It's dinnertime, and she's hungry! "Want to eat?" Sophie asks. Trix barks and wags her tail. Sophie scoops dog food into her bowl. Trix is two years old. A **veterinarian** told Sophie to use high-quality dog food that is right for Trix's age. The right food keeps Trix healthy and gives her the energy to play.

TREAT THEM WITH KINDNESS

Do you want to teach your dog a new trick? Choose a healthy treat. Dogs love treats, but don't give them too many! When your dog does something you like, reward your dog with kind words or a treat. If your dog does something you don't like, ignore the behavior. This is called positive training.

Some Border Collies have a weird job. They are official goose masters! When a goose goes on someone's property, these dogs are trained to chase them away. No goose poop for those people!

Some Border Collies have rough coats. Some have smooth coats. Both kinds of coats come in two layers: a **coarser** outer layer and a softer undercoat. Both coats protect the dog from harsh weather. Trix has a rough coat. Once or twice a week, Sophie brushes tangles, dirt, and mats, which are big knots, out of Trix's fur. Trix always rolls on her back to get belly scratches, too.

Border Collies don't need to be bathed often. But if they get muddy they'll need a bath.

Dogs need their teeth brushed just like you do. After Trix's coat is clean, Sophie grabs Trix's dog toothbrush and toothpaste. Sophie's toothpaste would make Trix sick.

FUN FACT
Border Collies have a hard stare. They can keep animals in line with one look.

"Bedtime," Sophie says after she brushes Trix's teeth and her own. Trix runs to Sophie's room and jumps onto the bed. Sophie laughs. "Okay, you can sleep here." She slips into bed and pets Trix's head as they both fall asleep. "Good night, Trix." Sophie feels lucky to have such a smart and sweet dog.

After reading the book, it's time to think about what you learned. Try the following exercises to jump-start your ideas.

THINK

FIND OUT MORE. There is so much more to dig up about Border Collies. What do you want to learn? Find out more on the American Kennel Club website. Or look for a Border Collie club in your area. You can meet people who love them as much as you do!

CREATE

ART TIME. Can you draw a Border Collie? Look up a cute picture and grab some markers and paper. Will your pup have a fancy hairstyle? Will it wear a fun hat? What is its favorite toy or game? Does it have a job? The sky is the limit!

SHARE

THE MORE WHO KNOW. Share what you learned about Border Collies. Use your own words to write a paragraph. What are the main ideas of this book? What facts from the book can you use to support those ideas? Share your paragraph with a classmate. Do they have any comments or questions about Border Collies?

GROW

HELP OUT! There are dogs near you that need care. Animal shelters can be great places to volunteer and hang out with pups. Contact a shelter near you and find out if you can help. Or can your family donate food or gear to help rescue dogs? Find out why dogs end up in shelters. Is there anything you can do to help them find homes?

RESEARCH NINJA

Visit www.ninjaresearcher.com/4712 to learn how to take your research skills and book report writing to the next level!

Research

SEARCH LIKE A PRO

Learn how to use search engines to find useful websites.

FACT OR FAKE

Discover how you can tell a trusted website from an untrustworthy resource.

TEXT DETECTIVE

Explore how to zero in on the information you need most.

SHOW YOUR WORK

Research responsibly–learn how to cite sources.

Write

GET TO THE POINT

Learn how to express your main ideas.

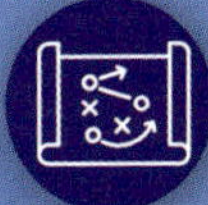

PLAN OF ATTACK

Learn prewriting exercises and create an outline.

Further Resources

BOOKS

Furstinger, Nancy. *Canine Athletes: Herding Dogs*. North Mankato, Minn.: Abdo Publishing, 2019.

Gagne, Tammy. *Dog Encyclopedias: Collies, Corgies, and Other Herding Dogs*. North Mankato, Minn.: Capstone, 2017.

Sabelko, Rebecca. *Awesome Dogs: Border Collies*. Minnetonka, Minn.: Bellwether Media, Inc., 2018.

WEBSITES

Factsurfer.com gives you a safe, fun way to find more information.

1. Go to www.factsurfer.com.
2. Enter "Border Collies" into the search box and click 🔍
3. Select your book cover to see a list of related websites.

Glossary

agile: the ability to move quickly and change direction easily.

ancestor: a person's or animal's parent, grandparent, and so on.

coarse: something that feels rough.

dominate: to go undefeated in a sport or other activity.

endurance: the ability to do something hard for a long time, like sprinting for a long distance.

gait: the way a person or animal walks.

instinct: a habit an animal or person is born with.

intelligence: the ability to learn and perform skills.

livestock: farm animals that are raised to make money.

manual: done by hand or paw. Today, most car windows are automatic. They don't need to be cranked by hand to open.

veterinarian: a doctor for animals.

Index

PHOTO CREDITS

The images in this book are reproduced through the courtesy of: Eric Isselee/Shutterstock Images, cover and p. 1; Maximillian Laschon/Shutterstock Images, p. 1 (paw prints); Erik Lam/Shutterstock Images, p. 3; DUSAN ZIDAR/Shutterstock Images, p. 5; Julia Zavalishina/Shutterstock Images, p. 5 (upper left); Eric Isselee/Shutterstock Images, p. 6; atnadro/Shutterstock Images, p. 7 (top); S1001/Shutterstock Images, p. 7 (bottom); Susan Schmitz/Shutterstock Images, p. 8 (top); gualtiero boffi/Shutterstock Images, p. 8 (middle); Jin Ah Kim/Shutterstock Images, p. 8 (bottom); dodafoto/Shutterstock Images, p. 9 (top); Zelenskaya/Shutterstock Images, p. 9 (bottom); Sheli Jensen/Shutterstock Images, p. 10 (top); Gary Perkin/Shutterstock Images, p. 10 (bottom); Makarova Viktoria/Shutterstock Images, p. 12; Eric Isselee/Shutterstock Images, p. 13 (left); Eric Isselee/Shutterstock Images, p. 13 (middle); Eric Isselee/Shutterstock Images, p. 13 (right); MirasWonderland/Shutterstock Images, p. 14-15; otsphoto/Shutterstock Images, p. 16 (top); Rita_Kochmarjova/Shutterstock Images, p. 16 (left); Eric Isselee/Shutterstock Images, p. 17 (top), p. 31; Vasyliuk/Shutterstock Images, p. 17 (bottom); Julia Zavalishina/Shutterstock Images, p. 18; Dora Zett/Shutterstock Images, p. 19 (top); Daxiao Productions/Shutterstock Images, p. 19 (bottom); Julia Zavalishina/Shutterstock Images, p. 20; cynoclub/Shutterstock Images, p. 21 (left);cynoclub/Shutterstock Images, p. 21 (left); Dora Zett/Shutterstock Images, p. 21 (right); mariesacha/Shutterstock Images, p. 22; otsphotoShutterstock Images, p. 23 (top); Sbolotova/Shutterstock Images, p. 23 (bottom); DenisNata/Shutterstock Images, p. 24 (top); Frank11/Shutterstock Images, p. 24 (bottom); Jose Luis Carrascosa/Shutterstock Images, p. 25 (top); Dora Zett/Shutterstock Images, p. 25 (bottom); Julia Zavalishina/Shutterstock Images, p. 26.

About the Author

Renata Marie is a children's book editor and author. She has also written a young adult novel and flash fiction. Renata loves sharing her stories with her mom's classroom and hanging out with her two overly curious cats and big lap dog, Takoda.